Interior Thoughts

Shelley "Silverwine" Sprecher - Hitch

Interior Thoughts

13 Days of Halloween

www.localgemspoetrypress.com

Table of Contents

Fantastical Frenzy

Beautiful green fades into glittery gold
Red rubies of crystal brilliance to behold
against the silhouette of splintered beam
standing tall, Wooded trees.

White, browns, yellow textured textile
Mimicking the radiant picture within
Summer breathes magnificent dreams
Radiance among the shortening days.

Long sunny days wash-out into visible grays
Beyond the once green pasture roll
Outside sights of bewitching fall.
Foreshadowing change to crispy wet variations
Previously bountiful fruit, looking to live again
planning warmth hibernation, beckons to retain
What brings flickering seasons that change
Anticipated dreams alter with glorious dye
The distance sight which bares the slumber,
colorful hues

Riding Blind

Riding through a portal of crystallized mist,
Fragmented shadows peering into a swirling
sliver,
Only perceiving a portion of what exist.
Hustling at a high rate of speed, cares to the
wind,
with the greatest feeling of being at ease.
Tail pipes rumbling, like a jet plane from
above,
The smoke envelops behind me, into a fluffy
white cloud.
Not caring what happens, a whole different
person while I ride,
Holding my head up in honest, arrogant pride.
Seeing a small segment of what is actually near,
Along on the back highway riding along, oh my
God a deer.
Know that if I try stopping it will only make it
worse,

Hitting the accelerator, choosing to press on,
there is no reverse.

Eyes squint through the tears running down,
that are shed,

All dreams you've envision flash, the thought
of what's still ahead,

Thinking the end is so near, can't see a way of
getting out

All knowledge of riding, can't help those
cranial shouts.

The glaze upon the blackened road

Only you can do this, you were once told.

Faith in your training, as a slick slide start to
shift,

If only you could have seen what was out there,
premonition, exists.

Pumpkins

Lines on my face, crisp curly ruffles on my
head, a hard knobby top growing up toward the
sky. Oh, man, someone grabbed me, I'm
leaving my comfortable bed, I wish I could see,
to wave goodbye to my friends.
There are so many voices around me asking
what they should do, I keep turning and
swaying if I had a mouth I think I would spew.
A poke and a prod, a shot, splitting headache.
Oh this awful pounding, am I the only one this
is happening to.
I feel so violated with hands all over me. My
inners and getting squished, I feel like my soul
is being eaten away.
Oh my words, bright light pierced through my
face,
The glare is tough to place. I see so many
different things a whole new life, a new view,
my life has been replaced.

There are so many things I just don't understand. I feel so out of place, from the sights, and smells that I'm so cold and open, shaking from a crisp breeze.

I see the shadows eating seeds like my life was taken out of me, my soul feels hollow.

The night has come so fast, I feel so lonely and blue. I wonder if I can roll out of here, so I can reunite with my old friends the one I grew up with.

Suddenly I get picked up, put on top of a cold corner. As I look down I see my friends, I wonder if they came to rescue me.

A light gets placed inside my empty shell, I feel so warm and calm,

I see so much better, thank you my new friends, I feel so filled with light and new friends are with me

Haunted House?

Every house that you pass has a story to tell.
Doesn't really matter the look, outer
appearance, a shell.
Each family is a conduit, in that certain place,
that they dwell,
They're the real culprits, who make a vortex to
their personal hell.
Each house has a past, has a distinct type of
aura.
Doesn't matter the type of abode, not even the
grass or the flora.
Every kin that settles in, creates their own astral
panic.
They are barbarous fools, those serenity
stealing bandits.
Every home that you see, is similar in many
ways.
New or old where they stand, every family
helps it slip away.

Each family that remains, haughty, rotten clues,
never really understanding the pea picking
rules,
Being good to each other, stop the hurt and the
pain, cheating and lying, the abuse it's just
insane.
Each home that you pass, has a door and history
attached,
Windows show through beautiful light, rooms
to dwell in with love, not so far fetched if you
pray to God above.
When you see a house, you think it may be
haunted,
You need to think again.
It's not the houses fault, but the people who
dwell within.

Bar Talk

Guy: Have you heard the story of the
 woman down the street.
She's a witch I can tell you, it's true from what
I have seen.
Woman: Is that a pick up line because I'm not
biting.
I'm sure you say that to many ladies you meet.
Why should I believe in witches and such? I'm
sure you are just looking for a woman with a
Mercedes.
Guy: Give me. Break, I think you have class, I
just wanted to tell you a tale. The reason I say
because I heard they are recruiting today and I
don't want you to fall victim.
Woman: So your kind of cute in your jeans and
your boots, do you really know what these
"witches look like? How do you know, I'm not
one of those, maybe we could go out for some
fun.

Guy: Oh, I can tell, witches are ugly and old,
believe me when I say you are beautiful in
every way. So please have a drink with me and
let the night just unfold.

Woman: Sounds good to me, I'll have a drink
and we will see, how this night will unfold.
The first one I'll buy, so come by my side and
together we'll have s dark stout.

Guy: I really can't believe you're talking with
me, now I'm starting to feel kind of funny. My
eyes are getting tired, fogging up in the back of
my head. What have you done to me honey.

Woman: I thought you knew, what I was to do,
since you know witches so well. I came down
from the house, at the end of the street, so I
could find my next meal.

Fireworks

Going off to bed, covered my head, looking so
forward to a beautiful tomorrow. Slipping off
into my dreams, where everything see me to be
moving. beautiful fireworks in the air, the
colors so crisp and clear.
I was enjoying the night so sweet, walking
down a unfamiliar street, look up at the tall
glass towers. Street light are all lined, everyone
was out to unwind, with many people embraced
and entwined.
When out comes a man, with a gun in his hand,
I stop to wonder, what he has planned.
Everyone disperses, with lots of bad words and
curses , I can not believe what is happening,
Then all over a sudden, I see my brother
running, over to where we are. A shot rings out
so very loud, into mass hysteria of the frantic
crowd.

My brother yells at that man, with the gun in his hand, saying "you wanted me, so come here". Shots are now fired, two hit a tire, as one grazing the head of my brother.

I can't believe the sheer power and speed, of what has happened now. Standing in awe, where is the law, I just crouched and cowered. With the more bangs of the gun, the whole scene is done, waking up in such terror.

I can't believe, the reality of the scene, so I go back to sleep or I tried. Hoping he's fine, I breathed with a sigh, that I was just having a bad dream.

Morning has comes, up with the sun, a beautiful day is upon me. The phone begins to ring, not knowing a thing, it just happens to be my brother.

He says " you won't believe, what had happen to me, I need a ride from down town. I was enjoying myself, not bothering anyone else, there is no way to excuse me. A short time later, there was a true hater, on my trail you see. A bullet grazed my head, I thought I was dead, and the gash felt like I was rubbed with a grater.

Lucky for me, I beat it with my speed, grateful
my life was spared. So get on the move, before
I start to loose, my mind in this crazy place.
They are releasing me now, just don't have a
cow, oh and how did you sleep last night?

Party Fun, Halloween Past

Halloween party from my past, I was always so
drunk and totally smashed.
I hated being me, I was so nerdy and never
could be myself I guarantee.
So I got loose, felt like I completely had my
mind to lose.
Handing my boyfriend Halloween parties, an
uneasy time, a heart tease.
He had to watch me slink and slither. I can't
imagine why he even bothered with me and the
liquor.
Being a gypsy, an awesome fortune teller.
Smoking a green so high while I really
portrayed someone more stellar.
Pushing voices down, drowning them out, not
really working in spite of myself.
Being so intuitive, second nature at best, more
with the liquid gold I can't past this test.

No matter how good I was for others, I was so ashamed of myself, very bitter.

He gave me a backbone, that liquid Jack sliding down, waiting to place me under my headstone.

I didn't know how I could live with out the drink at hand.

Giving me confidence more spirit than not, for me to have openness with that shot.

Why did he watch me, kiss everyone there, why couldn't he leave me drowning my sorrows, for I hated living my life especially for tomorrow.

Perfect Tree Sight

Perfect barren beauty bright, show me your
nakedness this moon filled night.
Your skeleton holds such perfect form, against
blue skies of windy storm.
In the house my eyes do look, upon the trees
and the icy brook.
Howling winds blow strongly against the glass,
this beautiful scene I hope will surely last.

Delusion

A fusion of delusion, please don't mind this intrusion.
Illusion of confusion, so part of societies inclusion.

Of fall

I so love the wind
It is so clear and quiet
It has a shy side
And full mighty attitude
When it roars I feel happy

Forbidden Fruit

Forbidden fruit hangs before me,
To hold it in my hand so firmly, to take a bite or
not let's see.
Suck it's juices, chew it's flesh,
let it come inside my mouth, Couldn't imagine
anything less.
Forbidden fruit tenacious and delectable,
To take a bite thinking it could be incredible.
Looks so rugged in appearance,
Just wanting to expose the concealed savors
within it.
To relish the pleasure of its pure nectar,
Hoping to have it dripping from my lips into
my tastebud receptors.
The ambrosial sensation excites my life forces,
I want to eat you, enjoy, devour and savor, I
can't ignore this.
Everyday so seemingly out of reach, making
you a part of me,

Alway I feel by the hand of God, a strike of sheer destiny.

Not there Scare

Nightmare nemesis harrows, what sounds do
you hear,
Imagined inside butterflies, those persistent
childhood fears.
Ghost and ghouls existence, once existed
beyond what you've known,
Heightening haunting senses stew inside, the
great unknown.
Terror transforms reality, everything seems so
true,
Menacing madness ensnares, engulfing you.
Anonymous anomalies dancing, upon
shadowed stretched walls,
Restless rhythmic tapping, are they the souls,
come to call.
Exposed echoing engagement , paralyzing your
body down,
Scared sweating sickness, awaken,
 with a gasp, not a sound.

About the Author

Shelley "Silverwine" Sprecher - Hitch has been on a long road of learning. As a modern Renaissance woman, Shelley is a poet, foodie, master story-teller, quilt artist, adventurer, health enthusiast, and soulful blogger. She doesn't shy away from any topic from the sky to below as well as that including the metaphysical and supernatural. When she is not traveling in truck or on her motorcycle, Shelley is artfully sharing herself with the world through her blog SilverWine.

Made in the USA
Monee, IL
22 December 2020